LABOR DAY

LABOR DAY

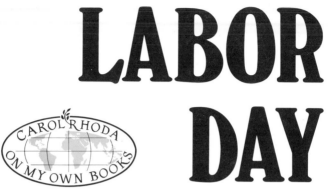

by Geoffrey Scott

pictures by Cherie R. Wyman

Carolrhoda Books

Minneapolis, Minnesota

to Emily
— *G.S.*

to Michele, for continued support and inspiration
— *C.R.W.*

LIBRARY OF CONGRESS CATALOGING IN PUBLICATION DATA

Scott, Geoffrey, 1952-
 Labor day.

 (A Carolrhoda on my own book)
 Summary: Describes the origin of the holiday
Labor Day, and how it spread from New York City
to other cities, finally becoming a national
holiday.
 1. Labor Day—Juvenile literature.
[1. Labor Day. 2. Holidays] I. Wyman,
Cherie R., ill. II. Title.
HD7791.S38   394.2′68   81-15485
ISBN 0-87614-178-5   AACR2

    1   2   3   4   5   6   7   8   9   10   87   86   85   84   83   82

Every year, on the first Monday in
September, we celebrate Labor Day.
Labor Day marks the end of summer.
It is celebrated all over the U.S.A.
But why is it called Labor Day?
What exactly are we celebrating?

We have not always had a Labor Day.
It's not a very old holiday at all.
The first Labor Day was held
only about 100 years ago.

It was not called Labor Day then.
It was not celebrated
all over the country, either—
only in New York City.

To labor means to work.

In 1882, many kinds of workers
lived in New York City.

Carpenters.

Bricklayers.

Furniture-makers.

Printers.

Most of them liked their work.
They were proud of their skills
and of the things they made.

But there were many things
that they did not like.
Most of them had to work long hours.
Many worked 12 or 14 hours a day!
And they didn't get weekends off.
They worked six, and sometimes seven,
days a week!
Often they worked in places
that were not safe.
Today if you worked 12 hours a day,
6 days a week, in a dangerous place,
you would be paid a lot of money.
But in 1882,
that was not the case.
Workers then were paid very little.

They were paid so little
that many families needed
their children to go to work.
So by the time they were 11 or 12,
many children were already working.

They were lifting heavy rolls of cloth
ten hours a day in a factory.

Or they were digging coal
six days a week.

No worker was happy
about these things.
But one person alone
couldn't change them.

So in the 1880s,

New York workers began to form

groups called craft unions.

Perhaps many people working together

could change the things

that one person could not.

At first each craft had its own union.

The bricklayers had their union.

The carpenters had theirs.

Then many of these small unions

joined together.

They formed a larger union

called the Central Labor Union.

The C.L.U. was, in turn,

part of an even larger group.

15

This larger group was called
the Knights of Labor.
The Knights of Labor
fought like the knights of old.
But they didn't fight with swords.
The Knights of Labor
fought with words and votes.
They fought to get children
out of the factories and mines.
They fought for better pay.
They fought for safer places to work.

Many of the workers in New York
had not been born in the U.S.
They, or their parents,
came from other countries.
In their old countries,
workers had special holidays.
Each craft had its own day.
The carpenters had their day.
The bricklayers had theirs.
The printers had theirs.
On their holiday,
the workers got the day off.
They went on picnics.
They held parades to show
how proud they were of their work.

But the U.S. had no workers' holidays.

Many workers in New York City

missed the old way.

They wanted a workers' holiday

in their new country.

They told their thoughts
to the Central Labor Union.
And on May 14, 1882,
the New York City C.L.U. decided
to hold a "monster labor festival."

The festival could take place

in early September.

The weather would still be warm then.

And it would make a holiday between

the Fourth of July and Thanksgiving.

There would be a parade and a picnic.

Everyone would have a good time.

They could show people

how proud they were of their work.

They could show how angry they were

about their working conditions, too.

We are not sure who had the idea

for the festival.

Some say it was Peter J. McGuire,

a carpenter from New York City.

Others say it was Matthew Macguire.
He was a machinist in New Jersey.
We do know that both men
worked hard on the festival.

Plans for the festival were made.

A park was found for the picnic.

The Union got permission

from the police to hold a parade.

Finally the festival date was set:

Monday, September 5, 1882.

By June 11, 1882,

the C.L.U. had sent out 20,000 tickets

for the festival.

Everything was ready.

There was only one question:

Would anybody come?

There had never been a day like this
in America before.
Would people be afraid
to try something new?
Would they be afraid
of losing their jobs?

July passed. Then August.
And still many craft unions
had not said whether or not
they would be coming.
Would the festival succeed or fail?
No one was sure.

At last it was September 5.
At 10:30 A.M. workers lined up
to start the parade.
The grand marshal
was William McCabe.
He was a leader of the C.L.U.
He was riding a fine horse.
He would lead the parade.
But when McCabe looked
at the marchers, his heart sank.
Only a handful of workers
were ready to march.

McCabe started the parade anyway.

But the labor festival

looked like a big flop.

Usually traffic stops for a parade.

But the workers' parade was very small.

No one stopped for them.

The marchers had to dodge around

streetcars and wagons.

McCabe had to work hard

to keep the little parade together at all.

32

Suddenly the marchers heard music.

It was coming from a side street.

It got louder and louder.

Who could it be?

It was the jewelry workers—

200 of them!

They came to join the parade.

And they brought their own brass band.

The music raised everyone's spirits.

A few blocks later,
the bricklayers joined.
They had a brass band too.
After the band
came some horse-drawn wagons.

In the wagons were brick steps,
walls, and window sills.
The bricklayers were proud
of their work.
They wanted to show it to everyone.

Soon more workers were coming.

Some had planned to join the parade
as it went.

Others were just late.

The parade got bigger and bigger.

Grand Marshal McCabe was now riding
in front of 10,000 marching workers!

Several bands were playing loudly.

Traffic came to a stop.

Thousands and thousands of people
were watching the parade.

They cheered and clapped.

They waved handkerchiefs.

Many of the workers
were wearing their work clothes.
The machinists wore their aprons.
The carpenters wore their tool belts.
The printers wore their paper caps.

Many of them were carrying signs.
The signs told everyone watching
what the workers wanted to change.

After the parade,

the marchers joined their families.

Then they went to Elm Park.

Nearly 50,000 people filled the park.

Everyone had brought picnic lunches.

Speakers talked about

how important the workers were.

They talked about how to start unions.

They talked about

ways to end child labor.

After the speeches, the bands played.

People sang and danced.

Fireworks went off.

It was a grand way

to end a grand celebration!

41

That first Labor Day in 1882

started out slowly.

The leaders worried that

no one would come.

But when the day was over,

they knew it had been a great success.

There was one thing they didn't know.

They had started a national holiday!

Workers all over America

liked the idea of a workers' holiday.

So the idea spread quickly.

By 1889, 400 cities had labor days

like the one in New York City.

Several states passed Labor Day laws.

Oregon was first.

Colorado, New Jersey, New York,

and Massachusetts soon followed.

By the 1930s, every state in the U.S.

celebrated Labor Day.

As Labor Day spread,

workers solved many of their problems.

Laws against child labor were passed.

Work days were made shorter.

The workers had been right.

By joining together into unions,

they were able to change things

that one person alone

could never have changed.

Workers today face new problems.

Factories are safer than they used to be.

But new machines cause

new safety problems.

So unions continue to work hard

to keep factories safe for their members.

Unions make sure

their members are paid well.

Unions help their members

in many ways.

We celebrate Labor Day
to honor American workers.
We think about how working hard
helps make our country strong.
And we remember
that all workers are important,
no matter what their job.